All Muslims
Shall Be Saved By Elijah
in the Bible

To order additional copies of this book, contact:
Xlibris
1-888-795-4274
www.Xlibris.com
Orders@Xlibris.com

ISBN: Softcover   978-1-7960-9976-8
       EBook   978-1-7960-9975-1

Print information available on the last page

Rev. date: 05/29/2020

All Muslims Shall Be Saved By Elijah in the Bible

Elijah Alexander

BOOK 1

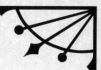

Heaven is great and hell is hot.

Choose you this day whom ye shall serve.

Why beholdest the beam in other people's lives and not their own?

Why shouldest thou considerest to do wrong?

When thou hast thee opportunity to do right?

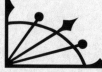

Dost thou know I'm a God of Judgement,

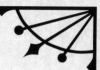

I still love thee.

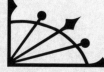

But I will not always chide with man.

I'm coming back soon.

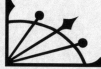

What a terrible day that will be
if thou knowest me not.

Can you imagine Gabriel with his instrument in the end time before Christ comes back.

What would you do?

Heaven is forever & Hell is forever

Printed in the United States
By Bookmasters